Reptiles

Leatherback Turtles

by Mandy R. Marx

Consulting Editor: Gail Saunders-Smith, PhD

Content Consultant:
Robert T. Mason, Professor of Zoology
J.C. Braly Curator of Vertebrates
Oregon State University

CAPSTONE PRESS
a capstone imprint

Pebble Plus is published by Capstone Press,
1710 Roe Crest Drive, North Mankato, Minnesota 56003.
www.capstonepub.com

Books published by Capstone Press are manufactured with paper containing at least 10 percent post-consumer waste.

Library of Congress Cataloging-in-Publication Data
Marx, Mandy R.
  Leatherback turtles / by Mandy R. Marx.
    p. cm. — (Pebble plus. reptiles.)
  Includes bibliographical references and index.
  Summary: "Simple text and photographs present Leatherback Turtles, how they look, where they live, and what they do"—Provided by publisher.
  ISBN 978-1-4296-6646-6 (library binding)
  1. Leatherback turtle—Juvenile literature. I. Title. II. Series.
  QL666.C546M37 2012
  597.92'89—dc23   2011024508

Editorial Credits
Kristen Mohn, editor; Kyle Grenz, designer; Kathy McColley, production specialist

Photo Credits
Alamy: Françoise Emily, 5, Michael Patrick O'Neill, cover, 13; Corbis: Frans Lanting, 1, National Geographic Society/ Brian J. Skerry, 7, 11, 19, Science Faction/Jason Isley -Scubazoo, 9; Getty Images: Science Faction/Jason Isley - Scubazoo, 15; Photo Researchers, Inc: Matthew Oldfield, Scubazoo, 21; Shutterstock: Fanny Reno, back cover

Note to Parents and Teachers

The Reptiles set supports science standards related to life science. This book describes and illustrates leatherback turtles. The images support early readers in understanding the text. The repetition of words and phrases helps early readers learn new words. This book also introduces early readers to subject-specific vocabulary words, which are defined in the Glossary section. Early readers may need assistance to read some words and to use the Table of Contents, Glossary, Read More, Internet Sites, and Index sections of the book.

Printed in the United States of America in North Mankato, Minnesota.
102011
006405CGS12

Table of Contents

Ocean Turtles

Leatherback turtles are the largest turtles in the world. These giant reptiles grow up to 7 feet (2 meters) long.

Leatherback Bodies

Leatherback turtles

live in the sea.

Their strong flippers

work like paddles

to pull them through water.

Leatherback turtles do not
have hard shells. Their shells
feel like thick, oily leather.
Ridges on the shells
help turtles swim swiftly.

A leatherback's favorite food
is jellyfish. Special spines
in the turtle's throat help it
swallow the jellyfish.

jellyfish

World Travelers

Leatherback turtles are found in the Atlantic, Pacific, and Indian Oceans. These world travelers swim thousands of miles in their lifetimes.

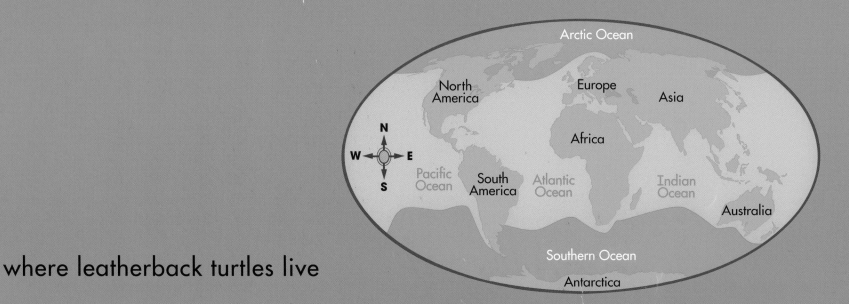

where leatherback turtles live

Leatherback turtles can keep warm in cool water. Swimming heats their muscles. Thick body fat holds in the heat.

Life Cycle

Females lay about 80 eggs in beach nests. In two months hatchlings crawl to the sea. Leatherbacks can live up to 45 years.

Leatherback Turtle Life Cycle

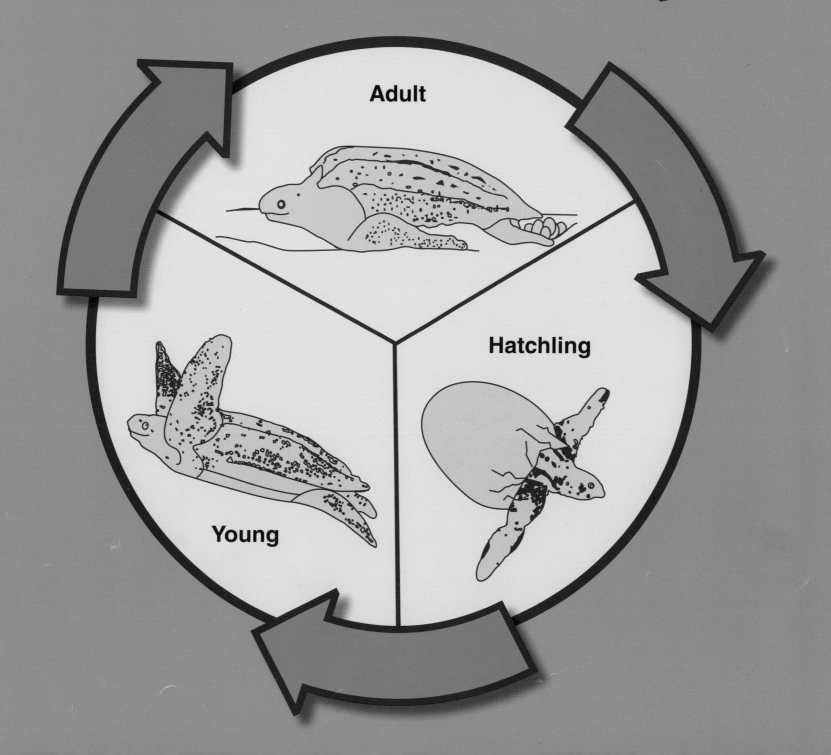

Threats to Leatherbacks

Leatherback turtles are
endangered. Cities were built
on their nesting grounds.
Many leatherbacks
die in fishing nets.

Leatherbacks also die from eating trash that looks like jellyfish. Keeping beaches and oceans clean will help leatherback turtles survive.

Glossary

endangered—in danger of dying out

flipper—one of the broad, flat limbs of a sea creature

hatchling—a young animal that has just come out of its egg

jellyfish—a sea animal that has a soft, almost clear body and tentacles

leather—animal skin used to make shoes, bags, and other goods

reptile—a cold-blooded animal that breathes air and has a backbone; most reptiles have scales

ridge—a narrow raised strip

spine—a hard, sharp, pointed growth

survive—to stay alive

Read More

Hall, Kirsten. *Leatherback Turtle: The World's Heaviest Reptile.* SuperSized! New York: Bearport Pub., 2007.

Sayre, April Pulley. *Turtle, Turtle, Watch Out!* Watertown, Mass.: Charlesbridge, 2010.

Wearing, Judy. *Sea Turtles.* World of Wonder. New York: Weigl Publishers, 2010.

Internet Sites

FactHound offers a safe, fun way to find Internet sites related to this book. All of the sites on FactHound have been researched by our staff.

Here's all you do:

Visit *www.facthound.com*

Type in this code: 9781429666466

Super-cool stuff! Check out projects, games and lots more at **www.capstonekids.com**

Index

Word Count: 176
Grade: 1
Early-Intervention Level: 18